Upward, Inward, Outward, Forward: Improving the 4 Dynamics of Your Small Group

Third Edition

Jim Egli

TOUCH® Publications, Inc.
Houston, Texas, U.S.A.

Published by TOUCH® Publications, Inc.
P.O. Box 7847
Houston, Texas, 77270, U.S.A.
800-735-5865 • www.touchusa.org

Cover design by Neubauer Design Group, Franklin, TN
Text design by Rick Chandler
Editing by Scott Boren and Randall Neighbour

International Standard Book Number: 978-0-9788779-4-1

All Scripture quotations, unless otherwise indicated, are from the *Holy Bible*, New International Version, Copyright © 1973, 1978, 1984 by International Bible Society.
Used by permission.

TOUCH® Publications is a division of TOUCH® Outreach Ministries, a resource and consulting ministry for churches with a vision for a holistic small group-based local church structure.

To download the presentation from our web site to facilitate this workshop in your church, visit our web site's "resource support" area. The presentation is password protected. The name and password you will need are: *dynamics* and *growth*.

Find us on the World Wide Web at www.touchusa.org

Upward, Inward, Outward, Forward: Improving the 4 Dynamics of Your Small Group

Table of Contents

Introduction

Small groups have captured the attention of Christian leaders around the world. We have known for some time that churches who base ministry on small groups are the fastest growing churches and are the most effective in reaching non-Christians with the Good News of Christ. Yet until recently, no one had studied what makes small groups grow. We did not know the answers to the simple question: Why do some groups thrive and grow while others struggle and stagnate?

Now our knowledge has dramatically changed. My friend, Joel Comiskey, statistically compared 700 small groups in seven different countries overseas. I took Joel's research tool and applied it to 200 groups in the United States. Joel's research overseas and mine in the U.S. revealed that the same dynamics make small groups grow around the world.

As I applied these principles in my own church's small group ministry and taught them to others, I struggled with how to summarize and communicate these new discoveries. A breakthrough came when I realized that the concepts that Joel Comiskey uncovered could be communicated in four words. Growing small groups practice four simple dynamics. They reach: Upward (in prayer), Inward (to experience community), Outward (to the lost), and Forward (in leadership multiplication).

Grasping these four principles and applying them *rapidly* accelerated the growth of my own small group and transformed the way I equipped others. This new workshop is based on these simple but powerful principles.

The equipping in this workbook will inform and inspire you but it will go beyond that. Its six lessons will move you from learning to application as you pray and form a practical plan for your own group.

At the end of the book, you will find an optional lesson in the Appendix that will help you integrate the four dynamics into your small group meetings.

I am excited about your potential and the potential of your group! Jesus has wonderful things in store for you. The four principles you will discover and apply are biblical, practical and proven. If you prayerfully reach Upward, Inward, Outward, and Forward, you will see amazing results.

Yours in Christ,
Jim Egli

Session

1

Capturing the Small Group Vision

Capturing a Vision for Small Groups

 Personal Reflection

Write answers to the questions below. After you have written down your own responses, turn to someone near you and discuss your answers with one another.

- Have you ever experienced a life-changing small group? If so, when and where?

- Why did the group have so much of an impact on you?

- What did the leader do that made him or her effective as a leader?

Write your discoveries from the group discussion of the above questions below:

- What makes a group life-changing?

- What can leaders do to make their groups impact others' lives?

The Small Group Vision:

The life appeared; we have seen it and testify to it, and we proclaim to you the eternal life, which was with the Father and has appeared to us. We proclaim to you what we have seen and heard, so that you also may have fellowship with us. And our fellowship is with the Father and with his Son, Jesus Christ.

- 1 John 1:2-3

Small Group Life Involves:

• _____ the life of Christ . . .

• . . . in _____ with one another

• _____ His life and fellowship to more and more people.

Small Groups:

• Are the best way to unite discipleship, caring ministry, and _____.

• Have a support and training system to encourage their life and growth.

• Encourage each small group leader to receive a _____ from God that fits within the overall small group ministry and missional vision of a local church.

Small Group-based Churches:

• Connect people through _____.

• Form groups as the base of ministry and mission for church.

• Connect group leaders to the church vision through _____.

• Seek to grow and multiply groups by _____ _____.

Small Group Leaders:

- Follow Jesus, the Good Shepherd.

- Serve as _____ - _____.

- Normally oversee groups of no more than _____.

    - Even Jesus chose not to pastor a multitude of people.

    - 12 is the optimal number.

A Small Group Leader's Job Description:

1. To strengthen the weak.

2. To heal the sick.

3. To bind up the injured.

4. To bring back the strays and to seek the lost.

5. To lead _____ and not _____. (Ezekiel 34:1-6)

How Does Someone Become a Small Group Leader?

1. Experience _____ _____ through active involvement in a small group.

2. Complete your church's required leadership training track.

3. _____ in a current group as an apprentice or a co-leader (1 Tim. 3:10).

4. Receive the blessing of your church's pastoral leadership by demonstrating faithfulness to the Lord, your church's leadership, and others.

Key Growth Factors

Extensive statistical research has been done by Dr. Joel Comiskey and Jim Egli on what factors contribute to small group growth. This research involved surveying 900 small group leaders in the United States and seven other countries. It compared information about the groups' growth with their personal information and behavior.

In all eight countries the same factors impacted group growth.

Now it's time for you to guess which factors make a big difference.

Small Group Leaders whose groups grow most rapidly . . .

Amount of Difference:	Big	Little	No
Are Married			
Are Single			
Are Well-educated			
Have an Outgoing Personality			
Are Younger			
Have Been a Christian a Long Time			
Have the Gift of Evangelism			
Have the Gift of Teaching			
Pray Daily for their Group Members			
Spend More Time Daily with God			
Set Goals for Group Multiplication			
Identify and Involve Potential Leaders			
Spend More Time with Group Members			
Follow Up on Visitors			
Spend More Time Preparing for the Meeting			

Dynamic & Healthy Small Group Ministry Involves:

- Reaching *Upward* to God.

- Reaching *Inward* to Build Body Life.

- Reaching *Outward* to Unchurched People.

- Moving *Forward* to Multiply Ministry.

The three-legged stool.

1. Prayer is the central element through which the other elements emerge. Our relationship with the Lord connects all of the dimensions and holds it all together.

2. We need all four elements or the stool will fall.

3. Without all four operating in a small group, it will _____.

4. With all four working together, there will be strength, life, and growth.

Small Group Assessment

This form will help you assess the effectiveness of your small group today. Answer the questions by circling a number on each continuum showing where you or your group falls on each scale. After you have responded to the questions, follow the instructions at the end of the form to see your results.

Upward-Connecting Your Group to God:

How many days each week do you pray for the other members of your small group?

0 Days	1-2 Days	3-4 Days	5-6 Days	7 Days
0	1	2	3	4	_____

How many minutes do you spend in devotional time with the Lord on the average day?

0-5	6-15	16-30	31-45	46+
0	1	2	3	4	_____

How many minutes does your small group spend in worship in its meetings?

0-4	5-9	10-14	15-19	20+
0	1	2	3	4	_____

How many minutes does your group spend in prayer during meetings?

0-5	6-15	16-30	31-45	46+
0	1	2	3	4	_____

How often does your group see wonderful and miraculous answers to prayer?

Never	Sometimes	Often	Very Often	Regularly
0	1	2	3	4	_____

Total: _____

Inward-Building Community:

How many times in the average four week span does your small group meet?

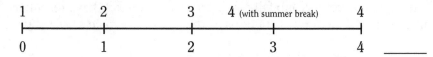

How many parties or fun activities has your group enjoyed together in the past three months?

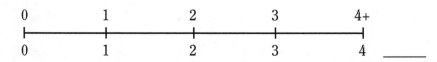

How many times have you invited group members to your home or a restaurant for a meal in the past two months?

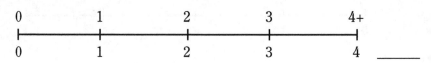

How often do most of your small group members sit together in congregational worship services?

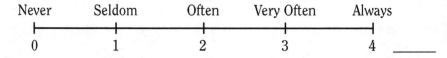

How often do you communicate with other group members by phone, email, cards or letters in order to encourage them?

Never	Sometimes	Often	Very Often	Daily	
0	1	2	3	4	_____

Total: _____

Outward-Reaching the Lost:

How often does your group take time in its meetings to pray for those that do not yet know Christ?

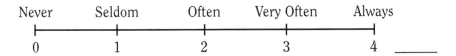

Never	Seldom	Often	Very Often	Always
0	1	2	3	4 _____

How many days each week do you pray for the salvation of unbelieving friends, relatives, neighbors, coworkers, or classmates?

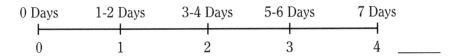

0 Days	1-2 Days	3-4 Days	5-6 Days	7 Days
0	1	2	3	4 _____

How many parties or fun events has your group enjoyed in the past three months that were targeted to appeal to unchurched friends?

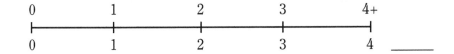

0	1	2	3	4+
0	1	2	3	4 _____

When a visitor attends your small group for the first time, are they followed up with a phone call, note, email message, or personal visit?

Never	Seldom	Often	Very Often	Always
0	1	2	3	4 _____

Does your group have a clear, dated goal for when it will multiply or branch out to form an additional group?

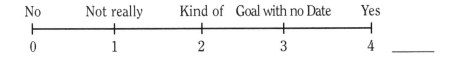

No	Not really	Kind of	Goal with no Date	Yes
0	1	2	3	4 _____

Total: _____

Forward-Multiplying Leaders:

How many individuals or couples in your group serve as apprentices or assistants right now?

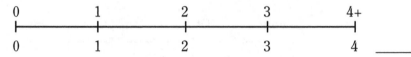

What percentage of your group members do you expect to lead a group at some point in the future?

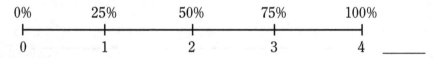

What percentage of the youth and adults in your group are involved in leading various parts of the meeting?

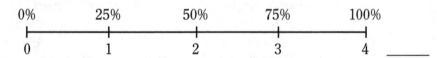

How often do your prayers for your group include a prayer for the multiplication of leaders?

Never	Seldom	Often	Very Often	Always
0	1	2	3	4

How many individuals or couples in your group do you expect to go through group leadership training in the next year?

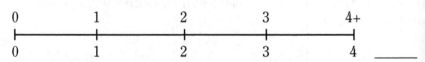

Total: _____

Enter your totaled scores from each of the four parts as dots on the chart below and connect the dots.

#	Upward	Inward	Outward	Forward
20				
18				
16				
14				
12				
10				
8				
6				
4				
2				

Your lowest score shows your most critical area for improvement.

Scores below 10 are cause for concern. Scores below seven indicate serious need and are cause for alarm.

Prayerfully consider the results of this form as you plan your next steps throughout this workshop.

Small Group Leadership Assessment Summary Form:

Please complete this form and give a copy of it to your pastor for review.

What were your four scores?

Upward: ____

Inward: ____

Outward: ____

Forward: ____

Are you currently a small group leader? Yes ____ No ____

If you are a group leader, please answer the questions below:

How many months have you led a group? ____ Months

Has your group multiplied since you became a leader? Yes ____ No ____

If so, how many times has it multiplied? ____

If so, how many months did it take to multiply? (Give an average if it has multiplied more than once.) ____ Months

Why Make Plans?

Commit to the Lord whatever you do, and your plans will succeed.
                                                          - Proverbs 16:3

Good plans begin with a pure devotion to God.

He reveals _____.

Without priorities, the "tyranny of the urgent" always takes over.

Small groups grow when they focus on priorities, not _____.

  • As one man said, "I had rather build a fence at the edge of a cliff
    than put an ambulance at the bottom."

When you hear God's "Yes" clearly, you will be able to say, "_____."

Session

2

Reach Upward:
How to Plug into God's Power

How to Personally Plug into God's Power

Christ is Our Life Source!

I am the vine; you are the branches. If a man remains in me and I in him, he will bear much fruit; apart from me you can do nothing.
                                                            - Jesus (John 15:5)

- If we remain, we will bear much fruit!

This is to my Father's glory, that you bear much fruit, showing yourselves to be my disciples.
                                                            - Jesus (John 15:8)

- To "remain" means to "_____, _____, or _____."

- Apart from Him, we can accomplish nothing. Ministry and leadership apart from Christ is like pushing a car that is out of gas, or using a mixer that is not plugged in!

- Listen and obey. _____, not _____, is the key.

Ideas to Personally Plug into Christ

1. Take _____ time with Christ . . .

- Daily time. Take time every single day following the Seven-Minute Rule.

> The *Seven-Minute Rule*: Taking at least seven minutes each day with God for the rest of your life.

- Generous time. If you are consistently taking daily time, begin taking a generous amount of time each day to enjoy God. You can determine what generous is for you right now in your life and walk with the Lord.

- Voluntary vulnerability. If you are stuck and cannot move forward,

  consider _____. This means going without food to focus more on prayer. It makes you feel weak and vulnerable. It is a way to get serious about prayer without waiting for problems to make you feel weak and desperate.

2. Pray consistently for the other members of your group. Statistical research by Joel Comiskey shows that leaders who pray for members six or seven days a week grow twice as fast as those who pray for members one or two days a week! (Even if you're not a leader today, you should still pray for your fellow group members each day. It shows you care.)

3. *Listen* to God. Just as Jesus did, take time to listen to God as you pray for the other members. Sit quietly and wait for God to speak to you for words of encouragement for the other person and He will!   *- Luke 22:31-32*

Personal Worksheet
Going Deeper with Christ

 Personal Reflection

How is God calling you to more fully abide in Christ?

What obstacle or obstacles have kept you from time with God?
Are there strongholds behind these obstacles that need to be dealt with
and repented of? (For example, materialism or people-pleasing may be behind
busyness.)

What is one thing that you would like to do to pray more specifically
for fellow small group members? What is the next step in fulfilling this
action?

After answering the questions above, share and pray with another person
nearby.

Ideas to Help You Plug into God's Power as a Group

1. Take a generous amount of time for prayer in group meetings.

   • _____ other dimensions of the meeting (such as worship or Bible study) to pray more. A quick prayer at the end of the meeting won't work!

   • Divide into _____ _____ for prayer, such as men and women, or groups of three or four. This maximizes personal sharing, prayer and ministry.

2. Schedule a "Half-Night of Prayer" every six to eight weeks. These nights consistently move groups to a deeper level in faith and expectancy.

   • You may need to schedule it on a night other than the group meeting to allow it to go a little longer than a meeting.

   • Consider fasting for one or two meals proceeding the evening of prayer.

   • Try using one of the two formats provided on page 25, then change it to make it better for your group.

3. Practice _____ _____ as part of your meeting. Ask God to show you the needs of the people who live on that street, in that neighborhood, or area of town. Invite God's Holy Spirit to work in power in that geographic area, and recommit yourself to minister to people's needs.

4. People always turn to God in prayer in times of _____. Fasting is a great way to put yourself into a crisis of sorts, so don't hesitate to organize a "hand-off fast" to get ahold of God or to see prayer answered. Each person takes a day and goes without breakfast and lunch, using the time to pray. Then, at dinner time the person calls the next person on the list and prays with them, then eats his or her evening meal.

5. In your group meetings, _____ how you are praying for others. This will encourage those who don't know how to pray.

6. Someone in your group should keep a prayer journal. Write in the request and when it was answered, and make notes of the specifics of how God answered the prayer. Then, when the group needs encouragement or on the last night of a meeting before multiplication, you can read all that God has done for the members of your group.

7. Schedule a brief, yet powerful _____ _____ to other member's homes.

   • 15-20 minutes in length; scheduled when it is convenient for the person receiving the visit.

   • This is not a social visit. Resist the urge to eat a piece of pie or drink a cup of coffee. You are there to pray for the household.

   • After you arrive, ask for any specific prayer requests. If the people who live in the house can't think of anything, that's ok.

   • Pray for needs or pray a blessing over them and their home.

   • Share a personal word of encouragement. You will find it helpful to write this out before you arrive if you don't know the person well. However, you should not read it to them. Don't worry, you'll remember it!

   • Be sure to ask about and pray for unbelieving friends. Ask God to give the person a clear understanding of how to pray and serve lost friends, family, coworkers, and neighbors.

8. Appoint an _____ _____ for the next four months of group life. This is a short-term role for a group member who feels called to help the group advance prayer in the group. He or she will remind the group of all the plans they have made for prayer and fasting and insure the group prays enough when they meet.

Half-Night of Prayer Samples:

Sample Agenda #1

7:00 Praise and Worship
7:15 Silent Confession
7:20 Prayers of Thanksgiving
7:30 Announcements
7:40 Blessing & Prayer for each person/couple
8:50 Break
9:00 Pray over names from the group's Blessing (outreach) List
9:15 Pray for anointing to reach the lost
9:30 In groups, pray for the church, nation, world
9:50 Prayer of Dedication of our Small Group
10:00 Refreshments and Fellowship

Sample Agenda #2

Part 1: Private Reflection (30 minutes)
Have each member pray privately through Ps. 103.

Part 2: Worship (30 minutes)

Part 3: Discussion (20-30 minutes)
Read Luke 11:5-13
1. Do you view God as being like the sleeping man or like a good Father?
2. How would you describe the person in vs. 8 who is seeking the help?
3. When was the last time you were like this before God?
4. What is the result of the boldness in vs. 9-10?
5. What does it make you feel like to be bold before God?

Part 4: Concert prayer for five minutes in each of the following areas:
(60 minutes) Worship and Praise to God; Prayer for self; Prayer for family; Prayer for church and its leaders; Prayer for non-Christian friends; Prayer for your nation.

Break

Part 5: Prayer walk the street where the host lives (30 minutes)

Part 6: Pray for one another (30 minutes)

Part 7: Pray over names from the group's Blessing List (30 minutes)

Part 8: Closing

Make a Plan to Plug into God's Power as a Group

Ask!

So I say to you: Ask and it will be given to you; seek and you will find; knock and the door will be opened to you. For everyone who asks receives; he who seeks finds; and to him who knocks, the door will be opened.

- Jesus (Luke 11:9-10)

Expect Miracles!

Did I not tell you that if you believed, you would see the glory of God?

- Jesus (John 11:40)

Pray and Plan with Others Now.

• Take time to pray, asking God to lead you and your group deeper into prayer. (If there are others at this meeting from your own group, do this exercise with them. If not, find one or two planning partners with whom you can do this and subsequent planning activities.)

• Write down two or three specific things that your group can do in the next two months to go deeper in prayer. Use the sample worksheet and blank worksheet on the following two pages as guides to help you make your plans specific and doable.

Sample Upward Worksheet

This page is included as an example. Develop your own Upward plan to connect your group to God using the blank planning page that follows.

Item	Dates	Who Will Do What?
Half-Nights of Prayer	12/3, 7:00-10:00 p.m.	Todd will plan agenda. Vicki will arrange worship and childcare.
	2/5, 7:00-10:00 p.m.	Jim will plan worship & communion. - Will ask Ike to lead second hour - Will ask Laponza to lead worship - Jan will arrange childcare.
Women's Thursday prayer luncheon	Try every other week for two months	Vicki will set up date with Joanna and Eno.
Fasting for Evangelism	Every Tuesday between New Years and Easter of Next Year	Leaders will fast two meals and invite others to join them fasting one or two meals to focus prayer on the lost. Jim will begin publicity at the close of the first half-night of prayer. (12/3)

Upward Worksheet

Develop a plan to deepen prayer. Work with others from your group. If you are alone, develop a working plan realizing that it will change as you confer with others from your group.

Item	Dates	Who Will Do What?

Important! As you add items to this worksheet, enter the dates on the planning calendar in the back of this booklet. This is the key to your success!

Session

3

Reach Inward:
Develop a Plan to Build
Community

Entering into Community

We proclaim to you what we have seen and heard, so that you also may have fellowship with us. And our fellowship is with the Father and with his Son, Jesus Christ.

- 1 John 1:3

Let the word of Christ dwell in you richly as you teach and admonish one another with all wisdom, and as you sing psalms, hymns and spiritual songs with gratitude in your hearts to God.

- Colossians 3:16

From him (Christ) the whole body, joined and held together by every supporting ligament, grows and builds itself up in love, as each part does its work.

- Ephesians 4:16

We Do Not Create Community, We Enter Into It!

(I pray) . . . that all of them may be one, Father, just as you are in me and I am in you.

- Jesus (John 17:21)

A Healthy Small Group is . . .

. . . much more than a once-a-week meeting! It's a "body" of believers experiencing _____ in Christ.

. . . A family, caring for one another and extending Christ's love. However, it's

not a _____ family. All families have disagreements and rub each other the wrong way. Healthy families work to find healing.

The Stages of Group Life

1. **Forming.** This "_____" stage is exciting. People are getting to know each other and are enjoying it.

2. **Storming.** In this "_____" phase of small group life, personality and value differences create tension. People are getting to know each other better and sometimes don't like what they learn about others!

3. **Norming.** Often called the "_____" stage. In this phase of group life, people have worked through many of their differences and are learning to love and appreciate each other's uniqueness. A sense of united vision can now the group forward if they are willing to do so.

4. **Performing.** Although outreach should be happening at every stage of group life, it often accelerates at this point in a healthy small group. For the group to remain intimate and effective, it must _____ _____ and start new group(s). If the group doesn't birth, it will slowly stagnate.

To Cultivate Community:

• Model _____, sharing your own needs.

• End meetings on time to allow for fellowship after the meeting.

• Open your home to others to hang out and for group meetings.

• Have fun and _____ _____ as a group once a month.

• Include group members in your _____ _____.

• Sit together, if possible, in your church's worship services.

• Share the stages of group life to help people have realistic expectations.

• _____ _____ _____ between meetings for no reason whatsoever.

• Enter into an accountable relationship with another member of your group.

• Appoint an _____ _____ to help cultivate community. This lperson's job will be to remind the group of the plans you have made today and keep the group on track.

31

Develop a Plan
to Build Community

 Personal Reflection

- In your opinion, what stage of small group life is your group in right now (forming, storming, norming, or performing)?

- What relational needs are in your group now (who needs a friend, help with a task, or should be invited over to your home for a meal)?

- What would you like to see happen in the next two or three months to deepen relationships in your group?

- Take a few moments to ask the Holy Spirit to build life-giving community in your group.

Make a plan to deepen community.

- Outline a possible plan to build community in your group on page 34.

Sample Inward Worksheet

Develop a plan to enter community in your group. If there are others from your group present at this meeting, work on this plan together.

Item	Dates	Who Will Do What?
Game-night	12/3	John & Cindy will host. Terry will organize finger-foods.
Send notes of encouragement	Once per month	Apprentices & core members
Send email twice per month to all members with email, sharing upcoming events and prayer concerns.	Begin 12/10	Jim
Invite Smiths over for Dinner	12/14	George & Iris
Christmas party & caroling	12/21	Todd & Jan
Birthday cake at the meeting for Terry	1/14	Theresa will bring cake.
Help Smiths move	1/30	John will coordinate.

Important! As you add each item to your worksheet, enter the dates on the planning calendar that you began earlier in this planning time.

Inward Worksheet

Develop a plan to enter community in your small group. Work with others from your group. If you are alone, develop a working plan realizing that it will change as you confer with others from your small group.

Item	Dates	Who Will Do What?

Important! As you add each item to your worksheet, enter the dates on the planning calendar that you began earlier in this planning time.

Session

4

Reach Outward:
Creating a Plan to
Mobilize Outreach

Effective Evangelism

 Personal Reflection

Answer the questions on this page as quickly as you can. Your first thought about each question is what you want to capture.

1. When you hear the word "evangelism," which of the following words or images immediately come to your mind? (Check all that apply).
   - ❐ Door-to-door witnessing
   - ❐ Passing out tracts on the street
   - ❐ Revival or tent meetings
   - ❐ Billy Graham
   - ❐ Caring friendship
   - ❐ Sunday evening services
   - ❐ Prayer
   - ❐ Talking
   - ❐ Listening

2. When you think of your own life, who was most influential in your decision to follow Christ?
   - ❐ Friend
   - ❐ Relative
   - ❐ Pastor
   - ❐ Co-worker or classmate
   - ❐ Complete Stranger
   - ❐ Other: _____

3. Which of the following words describe how you were influenced to Christ:
   - ❐ Warmth
   - ❐ Put-down
   - ❐ Cared for
   - ❐ Loving
   - ❐ Insensitive
   - ❐ Listened to
   - ❐ Manipulated
   - ❐ Other: _____
   - ❐ Other: _____

4. How many times did you hear the Gospel before you said "yes" to Christ? Circle one:

1 Time   5+ Times   10+ Times   50+ Times   Too Many to Count

5. Did you make one total commitment to Christ, or was it a series of commitments, setbacks and re-commitment?

6. How long did the process take?

7. How many people were involved in influencing you to receive Christ? Circle one:

1 person   2 or more   5 or more   10 or more

When you have completed your answers,
discuss them with someone near you.

Discoveries About
Effective Evangelism

Experience Reveals:

1. Many people have _____ mental pictures of evangelism.

    • They feel nervous or guilty when they think about "evangelism."

    • Yet most all Christians feel good about the way they themselves were evangelized!

2. The best evangelists are _____ _____ like you and me.

3. Active love is primary in drawing others to Christ. _____

    unbelievers and specifically asking them to _____ _____ creates a true friendship that reveals the Christ within a believer.

4. Evangelism takes time! While a few people accept Christ the first time they hear the Good News, most people find a relationship with God through Christ by watching the walk of a Christian and then deciding they like what they see.

5. _____ _____ are usually involved. Many unbelievers come to Christ when they consider a small group of Christians to be their closest friends. This is why its so important for you to introduce and involve your unchurched friends in your small group activities and relationships.

The three victories to win the war for a soul:
Win the person to you.
Win the person to your group or church.
Win the person to Christ.

Dave Earley, 8 Habits of Effective Small Group Leaders,
(TOUCH Publications, Houston, TX.), p. 40.

Biblical Images of Evangelism

1. The _____ Image

People in Scripture were often brought to Christ through friends or relatives.

- Andrew brought Peter to Christ (John 1:40-41).

- Matthew brought his pagan co-workers and friends (Matthew 9:10).

- Cornelius influenced relatives and fellow soldiers to receive Christ (Acts (10:22-24).

- Lydia and the Philippian jailer brought their families to Christ (Acts 16).

2. The _____ and _____ Image (John 4:37).

- Just like our personal experience, the Bible shows that evangelism takes time; it's a process; and multiple people are involved.

Ideas to Enhance
Your Outreach Efforts

1. Be Visitor Friendly!

- If possible, move your group from home to home to make it easier to invite friends. Your friends will come to your house and be far more comfortable than sitting in a stranger's living room.

- When you invite a friend to come to your group meeting:

    - _____ what will happen during the meeting *before* the meeting begins. Many unchurched people won't know what to expect.

    - Use simple song sheets for your worship time. Three or four easy-to-sing worship songs on a single sheet of paper will help visitors enter into worship with you.

    - Ask each visitor to your group for their phone number before they leave. Then you can call them and let them know where you are meeting next week, make plans to have them over for coffee, etc.

2. Keep Outreach Central

- Consistently "Share the Small Group Vision" for outreach and birthing new groups. It's easy to relax and forget why God has put you together.

- If your group has been together for at least four months, make planning and praying for the unchurched a high priority. Do these things right after your worship time to insure it does not get crowded out or forgotten.

- Work hard to get every member of your group trained in relational evangelism. If your church has a class or weekend event, attend it together!

3. Write a Mission Statement (do this in your next meeting)

- Is there a certain group of people or part of town that God has called your small group to reach?

- What do you want people who become involved in your group to experience?

- Write a simple mission statement that expresses the purpose of your group. (For example: The Bear Creek Small Group's mission is to reach an expanding number of families and individuals in West Houston and Katy, bringing them into a life-changing relationship with God and each other.)

- Review this mission statement often in your small group meetings so that you remain focused on God's purpose for your group.

4. Set Simple Goals

- How many people would you like to see come to Christ through the influence of your group in the next nine months?

- When would you like to multiply your group or launch a new group out of your existing group? This should be discussed and agreed upon by all the members of the group, then revisited frequently so you can pray about it and see it happen.

5. Utilize The Blessing List

Step 1: Prepare

- Photocopy the "Identifying Your Circle of Influence" master (one for each small group member).

- Complete it yourself.

Step 2: Present

- Distribute "Identifying Your Circle of Influence."

- Have each member write the names of unbelieving friends, co-workers, fellow students and neighbors.

- Have each person circle the names of their two friends who are probably most open to Christ.

Step 3: Make a Master List

- Put the two names from each list on the large "Our Blessing List."

- Have each member record the group's blessing list on the bottom of their page.

Step 4: Pray!

- Encourage each member to pray regularly for their own list and the group's list.

- Pray God's blessing and work in the lives of the group list in your weekly small group meetings.

- Love and serve these persons, individually and as a group.

Personal Reflection

- Is your group currently using a Blessing List?

- If "yes," how could you use it more consistently and effectively?

- If "no," write down on your planning calendar when you should introduce the list and begin using it. Before that date, enter a reminder to photocopy the necessary "Identifying Your Circle of Influence" page from the Blessing List tool.

6. Cooperate with God

- Are there adults or _____ close to your group or its members who seem open to God right now? If so, write their names below.

- Are there _____ _____ in your group with unsaved friends or relatives your group should reach?

7. Party! (Use food and fun to reach out and build relationships!)

• What _____ or holidays are coming up that would be
natural times to reach out and socially include non-Christian friends,
neighbors or coworkers in a fun activity?

• What are some of the interests of non-Christians in your group's circle of
influence? Do they like to go bowling, eat out or BBQ, watch or compete
in sports, etc.?

*After reviewing your answers to the above two questions, should you change
the social activities your small group has planned so that non-Christians can
be more easily included? Put these on your calendar.*

8. Tie into Church-wide Harvest Events

- Are there Christian concerts, performances or other entertaining events taking place in your church or community that small group members could invite unbelieving friends to attend?

- Write these events on your planning calendar. Then write down a reminder five weeks ahead of the event to pray for these events and to encourage small group members to invite receptive friends to them.

9. Appoint an Outward Captain

- Who in the group has a passion to build relationships with unbelievers and reach out to the lost? Write down this person's name or if he or she is here with you today, ask this person if they will serve in this capacity.

- The role of the Outward Captain is simple. Remind the group of all the plans made in the area of outreach, and insure the Blessing List is on the wall in the room where the group meets and that it receives the attention it deserves during prayer time.

Outward Worksheet

Develop a plan for outreach in your small group. Work with others from your group. If you are alone, develop a working plan realizing that it will change as you confer with others from your small group.

Item	Dates	Who Will Do What

Important! As you add each item to your worksheet, enter the dates on the planning calendar that you began earlier in this planning time.

Session

5

Move Forward:
How to Multiply Your Ministry

Multiply Yourself

And the things you have heard me say in the presence of many witnesses entrust to reliable men (Original Greek: persons) who will also be qualified to teach others.

- Paul (2 Timothy 2:2)

Follow my example, as I follow the example of Christ.

- Paul (1 Corinthians11:1)

 ## Ideas to help you discover your leadership abilities

1. _____ to host the group in your home, lead worship, coordinate refreshments, or tidy up the host home after the meeting. After all, this is *your* small group. Take ownership!

2. Ask God for _____ to see the incredible potential He designed within you and all He has planned for your life.

3. _____ _____ for opportunities to serve others. People follow those who have served them, and this is what true leadership is about (Luke 22:27).

4. When approached to serve as an _____, say "yes!" Chances are, you've already been doing everything required and it won't be hard or a lot of extra work. Do not let fear get in the way of God's call on your life.

5. Leading a small group is one of the _____ _____ a maturing Christian does, not the biggest thing he or she will do as they follow Christ into spiritual maturity. God has big plans for your life. Leading a group is the first step toward a life of ministering to others as a growing disciple of Jesus Christ.

Specific things a small group leader should do...

1. Ask your coach or pastor if it's the right time to invite a particular member to become your apprentice. They may have valuable insight to give you.

2. Give members responsibility _____ you invite them to be an apprentice or co-leader.

3. Pray and plan with your apprentice *and* _____ _____ in your group. A monthly meeting to plan the next six weeks works well.

4. Hold quick "debriefing sessions" after each small group meeting. Ask your apprentice and any other member who led a part of the meeting questions such as:

   • "On a scale of one to ten, how would you rate the meeting?"
   • "How could we have made the meeting better for everyone?"
   • "What did you see members and God do that encourages you?"

5. Apply the 4 to 1 rule when it comes to developing new leaders in your group: 4 times more encouragement than correction.

6. Ask your pastor if you can bring potential leaders with you to leadership meetings.

7. _____ responsibilities to your group members as soon as possible:

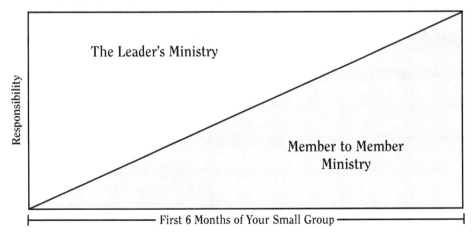

49

Multiply Your Group!

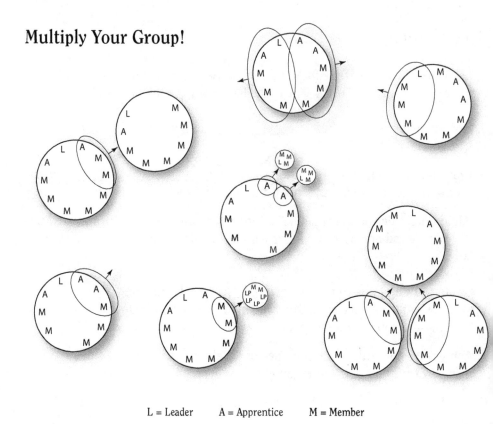

L = Leader   A = Apprentice   M = Member

Multiplication Principles:

- Keep the vision of multiplication continually before the group right from the beginning.

- Concentrate on raising up new _____. New groups will birth naturally.

- Lead group members to pray often, asking God if He would use them in birthing a new small group. Help members answer God's call and destiny for their lives.

- New groups are birthed by sending out a prepared leader or by the current small group leader leaving to start a new group.

- Protect the sense of community group members have developed. It does not have to be sacrificed for multiplication to occur.

Personal Reflection

1. What prevents you from becoming a future small group leader? (For those who already serve as group leaders: What prevents you from being the leader I feel God wants me to be?) Your answer(s) might include such things as:

    - Lack of time   - Unconfessed sin
    - Lack of training   - Simply don't want to do it.
    - Uncooperative spouse

   List your answer(s) here:

2. Are you willing to allow God to begin dealing with the item(s) you listed in #1 above? Circle one: Yes   No   Maybe

3. If your answer to #2 is "Yes," who could offer you prayer, support, and accountability as you allow God to work a transformation in your life?

   Write their name here: _____

   When and how will you will contact this person to ask for their help? _____

   _____

   Record information on the planning calendar at the back of this booklet.

4. Are you willing to ask God whether you should be a part of a newly birthed small group? Circle One: Yes   No

5. Are you willing to share your answers to the above questions with your planning group when you meet in a few minutes? Circle One: Yes   No

(It's O.K. and even important to be open and honest with the other members of your group concerning these things.)

51

Sample Forward Worksheet

List Names of Group Members*	**	Previous Experience and Strengths	Next Steps in Leadersh¡
(Jim)		Wants to be a leader as soon as possible.	Needs to learn how to relate to unbelievers.
Diane	√	Loves to talk with unbelievers. Very good learner.	Seek more flexible wor˙ schedule.
(Judy)	√	Very social. Has led worship effectively.	Should attend the next˙ small group leader training.
Ben		Very new Christian but willing to learn.	Allow God to work through some personal issues.

* Circle those who are interested in becoming a small group leader in the futur˙
**Make a check mark in this column to mark those who are willing to particip˙ in a new group when it's time to multiply the parent group.

Tasks to Assign Them	What Kind of Help is Needed from the Group	Goal Date [†]	Done
y for lost friends. ;anize the next up party to reach to friends.	Hang out with unbelieving friends of other small group members.	April 10	
;anize the prayer in. Lead icebreaker.	Prayer that boss will allow her to change her hours.	?	
d the Word portion he meeting.	Pray that husband will allow her to become a leader.	April 15	
et with group leader discuss issues that d him back.	Encouragement	June 1	

[†] When you have completed your worksheet, enter the dates on the planning calendar in the back of this booklet.

Forward Worksheet

List Names of Group Members*	**	Previous Experience and Strengths	Next Steps in Leaders

* Circle those who are interested in becoming a small group leader in the futur

**Make a check mark in this column to mark those who are willing to participa in a new group when it's time to multiply the parent group.

Tasks to Assign Them	What Kind of Help is Needed from the Group	Goal Date[†]	Done

† When you have completed your worksheet, enter the dates on the planning calendar in the back of this booklet.
[The small group leader will serve as the Forward Captain]

Session

6

Putting Your Plans into Action

Refine Your Plans

God Says to Refine Your Plans with Others

For lack of guidance a nation falls, but many advisers make victory sure.
- Proverbs 11:14

Plans fail for lack of counsel, but with many advisers they succeed.
- Proverbs 15:22

Make plans by seeking advice; if you wage war, obtain guidance.
- Proverbs 20:18

 ## Who Can Help Shape Your Plans?

1. Your leader, apprentice, or spouse.

2. Use the worksheets and/or calendar as starting points.

3. Your small group coach or pastor over small groups should know about your plans for two important reasons:

- They will be impressed by your work and encouraged that you have made plans to grow as a group.

- They know of church events and other important considerations that can help your plans succeed.

4. Group members who were not here with you today for the workshop should help refine individual parties and outreach events.

Next Steps

Refine Your Plans.

• With whom do you need to confer to finalize your plans?

• When should you make appointments to meet with them? (Write down tentative times on your planning calendar).

 ## Personal Reflection

• What two events that you planned today are most important?

• What are the next steps in implementing these activities or events? (Enter these next steps on the calendar.)

• What is one thing that you sense God saying to you today?

• What would you most like prayer for as you consider the needs in your small group?

Discuss Your Answers and Pray!

• Take time now to discuss your responses to the above questions and to pray together.

• From the discussion above, enter the key action items on your calendar.

Appendix

A

Incorporating the Four Dynamics in Your Small Group Meetings

Moving Upward, Inward, Outward and Forward in Your Small Group Meeting

A Recommended Format for a 90 Minute Small Group Meeting:

Portion of Meeting	Explanation	Flow
Welcome • 10 Minutes	Easy to answer icebreaker question that invites involvement from everyone.	You to Me
Worship • 15 Minutes	Simple worship that focuses on the Lord.	Us to God
Word • 25 Minutes of Study • 25 Minutes of Ministry	Interaction and application of God's Word, followed by ministry to one another.	God to Us
Witness • 15 Minutes	Planning and Prayer for Outreach.	God Through Us

Tips:
- Vary the format of the meeting. Do not get into a rut!
- Delegate different parts of the meeting. This leads the group Forward.
- Offer snacks before or after the meeting to promote fellowship.
- Flow naturally in and out of the various parts of the agenda.
  - In other words, do not say, "For our icebreaker tonight . . ."
  - Just discuss the topics without making the meeting feel formal.
- Start and end your meetings on time.
- Relax. If you're not having fun, you're not doing small groups right!
- Be Personal. Share your own feelings and thoughts and others will too.

Follow These Simple Principles:

Welcome
- Use non-threatening questions that can be easily answered.
- Go around the circle (avoid "popcorn" answers).
- Whoever asks the question answers it first.
- Example: "What is your favorite food and when did you last eat it?"
- Excellent stand-by question: "What was the most significant thing to happen to you since we last met?"

Worship
- Sing two or three familiar and easy-to-sing worship songs.
- Do not try to reproduce large group worship (lose the overhead projector).
- Prepare song sheets with just the songs you're singing that night.
- Be creative. Worship also includes: prayer, sharing praises, reading scripture etc.

Word
- Facilitate _____; teaching and preaching happen elsewhere.
- Ask open-ended questions.
    - Not: "What did Peter do to deny Christ?"
    - Rather: "What do you do when you are in a situation like Peter's?"
- Simple questions to ask:
    1. What stands out to you in this passage?
    2. What seems to be the main point?
    3. Can you illustrate this truth from an experience in your life?
    4. What is God saying to you right now?
- Encourage and model vulnerability.
- Allow plenty of time for prayer and quiet times to respond to God.

Witness
- Plan outreach events and nail down ____ will do ____ by ____.
- Pray for the people on your Blessing List.
- Discuss ways to serve your non-Christian friends.
- Frequently speak of branching out with a new group as leadership develops.

Improving Your Small Group Meeting

Pray together with others from your group or church. Then discuss the following questions and note the actions to take on your calendar.

1. What can you do to improve worship and prayer in your group?

2. What can you do to deepen the level of intimacy and sharing during meetings?

3. How can you make outreach more central to your group meetings?

4. What should be done to involve more members in the facilitation of your meetings?

Appendix

B

Calendars

#1

Year:

Month:

Review these plans with your coach or pastor to get his or her ideas and approval. Have them initial each page of your plan.

	Sunday	Monday	Tuesday	Wednesday	Thursday	Friday	Saturday

#2	Sunday	Monday	Tuesday	Wednesday	Thursday	Friday	Saturday
Year:							
Month:							
Review these plans with your coach or pastor to get his or her ideas and approval. Have them initial each page of your plan.							

	Sunday	Monday	Tuesday	Wednesday	Thursday	Friday	Saturday
#3 Year: Month: Review these plans with your coach or pastor to get his or her ideas and approval. Have them initial each page of your plan.							

	Sunday	Monday	Tuesday	Wednesday	Thursday	Friday	Saturday
#4 Year: Month: Review these plans with your coach or pastor to get his or her ideas and approval. Have them initial each page of your plan.							

Fill-in-the-blank Answers

Page 7 - Experiencing; fellowship; Extending; evangelism; vision; relationships; coaches; reaching unbelievers

Page 8 - under-shepherds; gently; harshly; community life; Assist

Page 10 - stagnate

Page 17 - priorities; emergencies

Page 20 - dwell: abide; rest; Obedience; activity; consistent

Page 21 - fasting

Page 23 - Minimize; smaller groups; prayer walking; crisis

Page 24 - share; prayer visits; Upward Captain

Page 30 - community; perfect

Page 31 - honeymoon; conflict; community; branch out; transparency; eat together; everyday activities; Call one another; Inward Captain.

Page 38 - inaccurate; ordinary Christians; Serving; serve you; Multiple people

Page 39 - Friendship; Sowing; reaping

Page 40 - Explain

Page 43 - children; new Christians

Page 44 - birthdays

Page 48 - Volunteer; faith; Pray daily; apprentice; first things

Page 49 - before; core members; transfer

Page 50 - leaders

Page 63 - discussion; who; what; when

Excellent Small Group Resources

The Pocket Guide to Leading A Small Group
by Dave Earley and Rod Dempsey
This powerful little book has 52 ways to help you adopt the practices of a healthy small group leader. By reading a few pages each week and practicing what you learn, you'll be surprised at how you and your group will grow!

Turning Members Into Leaders
by Dave Earley
This resource explains how to turn members into leaders who will say "Yes!" to leadership when you pop the question. The secret to developing leaders is to train them to lead *before* you ask them to lead. Want to know which areas in which they need experience so they'll be ready? It's all found in this book!

Leading From The Heart
by Michael Mack
Recharge your ministry and prevent burnout! Powerful small group leaders share a common trait: a passionate heart for God. They know their priorities and know that time with Him is always at the top of the list. This book will renew leaders' hearts, refocus their priorities and recharge their ministry.

8 Habits of Effective Small Group Leaders
by Dave Earley
The way to help people in your group discover and embrace personal transformation is to do some specific things *outside* your small group meeting. This best-seller is incredibly practical in nature, and will help you dream, pray, invite, contact, prepare, mentor, fellowship, and grow!

A Pocket Guide to Coaching Small Groups
by Randall Neighbour
This short, pocket-sized book does an excellent job of illustrating the importance of friendship in the coaching role. It's easy to read and great for busy coaches. If they just won't read, hand them this booklet.

Community Life 101
by Randall Neighbour
When people join your group, do they really understand what being a part of your group requires? The lighthearted and meaningful personal stories in this pocket-sized book drives home the fact that healthy small group life requires relationships outside of the weekly meeting and participation and transparency during meetings. If your members just show up once a week, this little book will help them adopt community life.

All of these titles and dozens of other excellent small group leadership resources are available at a special discount by buying directly from the publisher. Don't pay retail!

Order Toll-Free from TOUCH® Publications, Inc.
1-800-735-5865 • Order Online: www.touchusa.org